A CONCISE GUIDE TO NEWSPAPER FEATURE WRITING

E. J. Friedlander
University of Arkansas at Little Rock

UNIVERSITY
PRESS OF
AMERICA

LANHAM • NEW YORK • LONDON

Copyright © 1982 by

University Press of America,™ Inc.

4720 Boston Way
Lanham, MD 20706

3 Henrietta Street
London WC2E 8LU England

All rights reserved
Printed in the United States of America

Library of Congress Cataloging in Publication Data

Friedlander, E. J.
   A concise guide to newspaper feature writing.

   1. Feature writing. I. Title.
PN4781.F7   808'.06607021   81–40648
ISBN 0–8191–2115–0   AACR2

A Concise Guide To Newspaper Feature Writing

Contents

The Feature Story: What Is It?....... 1
Patterns vs. Formulae................ 7
Special Feature Writing Techniques....11
Twenty Five Story Types..............13
Feature Leads........................45
Postscript...........................49

KRAUSKOPF MEMORIAL LIBRARY
DELAWARE VALLEY COLLEGE OF SCIENCE AND AGRICULTURE
DOYLESTOWN, PENNSYLVANIA

INTRODUCTION

If you're a typical college journalism student, after graduation you'll find a job (if you're lucky) on some small newspaper in the boondocks.

The city editor there may not be at all like those sharp-tongued but patient editors you've been told about in journalism classes. Your first city editor probably will not have time to sit you on his gnarled knee, adjust his green eyeshade and carefully explain to you how your story could have been better written.

As a matter of fact, your first city editor may ignore you because he's too busy, he thinks you are beneath human communication or he believes you are a threat to his job.

So there is the distinct possibility that you may not learn too much from him other than that you want a better job and more money the second time around.

But despite his unwillingness to teach, your city editor will expect quality performance from you. And chances are that the city editor will tell you to "go out and do a feature" in your first week or two on the job. The feature probably will be about some elderly woman who thinks she owns a talking cat.

Hopefully, this guide will help you make that first talking cat story a little more acceptable, and you first editor a little more bearable.

THE FEATURE STORY: WHAT IS IT?

Two young reporters sit in the blackened corner of a bar, conveniently located a few yards away from the office of their small, daily newspaper. It's 4 p.m., the paper has hit the streets and the reporters are dissecting the day. Sipping beers, they talk.

"Edwards!" says Mann. "I can't get over what Edwards did today."

"You mean the feature story on the new movie theater..." asks Barr.

"Yeah," says Mann, a short, black-haired reporter in his late 20s. "That feature on the new movie theater."

Barr, a tall, lean reporter with a wisp of a mustache, plays with his beer mug. "Mann, it was good. Let's face it."

"I know," Mann groans. "That isn't the point. I know it was good and that's what I can't get over. Okay, he's sent out by the news department for the advertising department to do a routine puff piece on this theater. Am I right? Routine. Just an ordinary theater. Now what would you have done with that assignment?"

"Oh," says Barr, "I would have talked to the theater manager, looked the place over, and..."

"And you would have tried to get an angle on some new equipment in the theater or the management's policy on X-rated films," chimes in Mann. "Me, too. But Edwards walks in, starts talking to the projectionist and finds out that he hates to show war movies because he's a former prisoner of war who just happens to have won the Congressional Medal of Honor."

"It was good," offers Barr.

"It was great," returns Mann. "That guy could be sent out to do a story on the pet of the week and come back with a Pulitzer."

Newspaper feature writers don't have to come back with a prize winning story every time they leave the office, but they do have to have the ability to ferret out drama and irony in the most prosaic settings.

Take Edwards, for example. He could, as Barr and Mann suggested, merely have asked the theater manager routine questions and returned with a routine feature story about the routinely new projector or routinely adequate sound system the theater had installed. That approach would have satisfied the advertising department and probably the news department, too.

Instead, Edwards chose to look for the human angle in an otherwise dull setting, a new movie theater, just like 14,000 other movie theaters in the United States.

Edwards found that human angle, because he was curious, energetic, talkative and thorough. He found his angle because he was also intelligent enough to sniff out human drama from a story that, on the surface, let out only the slightest whiff of an odor.

Edwards, indeed, had interviewed the theater manager about the projection and sound system. But he didn't stop there. He wanted to see the new projectors. In the projection booth, he noticed the operator had difficulty bending over. Edwards asked the projectionist if he had arthritis and was told the pain came from a war wound From there, the conversation festered rapidly, from wounds to war movies to the Medal of Honor.

Laziness or lack of curiosity would have cost Edwards his story because the story was out of his way. It wasn't convenient; it wasn't in the manager's office. Timidness would have also cost Edwards the story because the projectionist did not volunteer his feelings--he had to be asked.

Edward's feature story was a type of Case History, more specifically, a Personality story. Features come in a variety of shapes and types. They range from Case Histories like the POW projectionist to New Business stories. They're different from news stories in several ways.

News stories are supposed to inform. Feature stories entertain as often as they inform.

Features also usually lack the urgency, the "read it all now," of a news story. And if these differences weren't enough, feature stories also happen to be written differently than news stories. How? Well, that's a hard question. If that sounds evasive, it is because no reporter who has written a textbook has ever quite been able to briefly and adequately explain how a feature is written.

Usually features are written in a narrative style rather than the traditional inverted pyramid used in news stories. The inverted pyramid style of newswriting, as you probably know, began to evolve in the early days of the Civil War. The stories surrounding the development of the style are part of the journalistic legend, but usually suggest the style was championed by war correspondents who were afraid that telegraph lines or other methods of communication from the war front might be disrupted before the news story could be completed. The answer to the potential disruption, so goes journalistic legend, was to write the story with the most important facts first, the less important facts second, and so on until the story was completed.

The news story, then, is written in a declining order of importance, called the inverted pyramid, so that it can be easily edited. The feature story, if it must be cut, should be chopped from the middle rather than the end. The feature, like a novel, has a beginning, a middle and an end. If the end is cut, the story just stops.

In addition to all this, features are heavy with human interest, color, description and characterization. In general, news stories are not. Features are waves of emotion in the journalistic sea of serious, fair and balanced reporting.

News and feature stories seem to have evolved at different times in history. News stories, obviously, are as old as news, but modern news story style dates to the mid 1800s. Feature stories probably can be traced back to the New

York penny press of the 1830s when readers began to demand more entertainment from their newspapers. However they came to be, modern features tend to divide themselves into categories of (1) news features, which must be printed rather quickly (though not necessarily immediately.) and (2) time features. Time features do not have to be used at any particular time. Like frozen hamburger, they'll keep for months without spoiling.

News Features:

News features usually have a news peg, some news event to which they can be tied. They are often sidebars, short features which explain in detail a part of a major news story. The sidebar may explain, for example, the atmosphere of a plane crash scene while the accompanying major news story, often on the same page, gives the reader the basic facts of the crash.

Take, for example, that plane crash story. The major news story would give the basic facts of the accident while the feature sidebar might picture the attitudes of the rescue team recovering the twisted, torn bodies. (Bodies are always twisted and torn in plane crashes and feature stories.) The news story would be bare and precise; the feature would be charged with emotion, color and description.

News features which are very short--only one or two paragraphs--are called brighteners. Brighteners need not always be bright, or upbeat, but they are traditionally called that.

Another common type of news feature story is the explanation piece--called a Backgrounder or Behind-the-Scenes story--which explains to the reader things he has never understood (how an atomic power plant will actually make the electric blender work) or events he has never experienced (the terror of jumping a motorcycle over 26 parked trucks). These stories are usually tied to some timely news peg (for instance, the grand opening of the atomic power plant), but also may be used as time features.

Personality features (a type of Case History) usually rip open the underside of an entertainment, political or sports personality and can be a news feature when they are tied to a news event. If the U.S. senator from your state is in your town for a speech, a Personality feature about him would have its own news peg--proximity to readers. If, however, you meet the senator on a plane on your way home from vacation, the story will be harder to write because you have no news peg to your town. The story can still be written, of course, but it would have to be treated as a time feature.

Time Features:

Time features are stories which can be run in the newspaper at almost any time, including never (which is exactly what happens to badly written time features). Time features can be brighteners, personality pieces without news pegs or any of the other story types listed in the fourth part of this guide. They must be able to be used at any time and should, in addition, have some traditional elements of news interest for the reader.

These elements of interest include proximity to the reader (the farmer who lives on the outskirts of town and raises warthogs); unusualness (the warthogs will do here, too); importance to the reader (how inflated beef prices have caused the widespread use of soybean hamburger in your town) and prominence, or the ability of the reader to identify or recognize participants (the town dogcatcher who stops work to watch re-runs of "Lassie" on television).

Timely or timeless features depend upon top writing skills as well as ideas. Ideas come with imagination. Good writing depends on the mastery of basic techniques, story types and lead variations.

PATTERNS VS. FORMULAE

Good feature writers are treasured by their city editors. They are treasured because they are versatile, like Dr. Jekyll and Mr. Hyde. They're versatile because small newspapers, being small, can't afford feature writers who aren't also reporters and layout people. On small papers, feature writers are also usually photographers. The feature writer-reporter is then, essentially, a switch hitter, capable of batting away at ordinary news stories with workmanlike effort and also blasting off an occasional home run with a dazzling feature story, with pictures, to boot.

Because they usually start their professional lives as straight news reporters, feature writers know all about journalistic formula writing. If you ask a veteran beat reporter if his stories repeat themselves, he'll probably grumble, ask you guardedly if you are from "Editor and Publisher" and then admit to duplication.

Admitted or not, it's a bare fact that much newspaper writing, including features, is pattern or formula effort. That's one reason reporters start to drink, or at worst, become city editors. News stories on weeklies and small dailies (and even a few medium sized ones) are all too often written with one of several traditional leads, dressed up with tired transitions and trimmed out with bits and pieces of material in a declining order of importance. That's what a formula is, a routine, patterned way of doing something. And that's precisely the way many accident, crime, speech and meeting stories are written, not to mention obituaries and family living material.

Feature stories, however, can't quite be handled with this totally cut and dried news formula. They do have repeating patterns, like news stories. Repeating patterns, however, shouldn't prevent feature stories from glistening anew with glitter every time they are written, even if the story is the tenth one your paper has run in that many years about the local man who invented the plastic cup or the town drunk who used to be the mayor of Kansas City.

The difference between the routine news story

and the feature story is the difference between a craft and an art.

A house painter can master his craft in several years. Each house requires a different, yet similar treatment. Paint must be chipped, new paint must be applied. Each house requires slightly different degrees and kinds of work, but the work is done according to a rough formula. The formula used for house painting can, figuratively, be applied to simple news stories. The journeyman newsperson regularly uses such formulae for his stories of fatal auto accidents, cats up trees, murders, meetings and speeches.

Features, however, are more like a painting than a painted house. Features can be artful, rather than merely craftsmanlike. Even artful features, though, share some characteristics with house painting and news stories. For instance, feature stories use repeating style techniques, story and lead types. Even if the feature writer freely mixes these techniques and types while painting his word picture, he is exercising creativity. This creativity separates the feature story from the routine news story, and most particularly, from house painting.

Thus the student of newspaper feature stories should note that they do not have totally repetitive formulae. They do often repeat patterns of technique and type. These repeating patterns should be studied in much the same way an art student studies the brush strokes and paint mixing techniques of the masters. Art students claim that after a couple years of studying and imitating technique and style, personal technique and style usually bloom.

Studying the technique and style of good newspaper feature writers probably will lead first to imitation, then to development of your own style. Pure imitation is less than craftsmanship. Creative intermixture of techniques, story and lead types will put your feature material several notches above routine craftsmanship. Art? Maybe not. Good reading? Yes.

Because many reporters consider feature writing more creative than straight news, the feature assignment is usually the high point of any reporter's day (providing he knows how to write a feature). Reporters on daily papers, even the worst hacks, look forward for the chance to get out of the office and away from the routine of councils, cops and courts to create images in print, to chomp down on a good feature story.

On afternoon (called P.M.) papers, where working hours are usually from 7:30 a.m. to 4:30 p.m., afternoons are ordinarily saved for digging up feature material. Usually, after the paper's deadline (it varies from 10:30 a.m. to 1:30 p.m.), reporters charge out of the office to work on feature pieces. Beat reporters, of course, have less time to do features and on a large daily may never do one.

On small morning (A.M.) papers, working hours are different, but the procedure is about the same. A.M. staffers generally work from 2:30 to 11:30 p.m., with a deadline usually around 7 p.m. and the evening hours saved for gathering feature material.

As a rule, features for A.M. papers are usually a little easier to cover because the reporter can catch his subject at home. P.M. staffers obviously have to find their subject at work sometime after lunch (which may not be as easy as it sounds if the story is about one of those types who doesn't work regular hours).

A.M. or P.M., most reporters agree that the well written feature story livens their day, makes their job seem worthwhile. It's the one time, they say, when they can throw a rock through the window of journalistic written-alike, look-alike news stories.

SPECIAL FEATURE WRITING TECHNIQUES

Good literary techniques are common to most good feature stories. These special techniques if used sparingly, can add power to your story, help it read better. For a more complete list, check any good guide to composition.

Anaphora: The writer repeats words or ideas for impact. Example: He lived hate, he breathed hate, he spoke hate.

And Chain: This frequently used device uses repetition of the word "and" for effect. Example: He graduated from high school and joined the police force and was a good cop, they say, and was shot to death last Saturday night for his trouble.

Circle Technique: Most newspaper feature stories use this approach to one degree or another. The circle technique requires that the story begin and end with the same idea, phrase, question, statement or description. The technique gives a feature unity and wholeness. Example: (A STORY ABOUT THE RECORD INDUSTRY) A finger punches a button. Reels on the expensive 16-channel Ampex tape recorder begin to move. The needle on the VU meter jumps. Sound is being recorded. (THE FEATURE CONTINUES WITH A NARRATIVE OF A ROCK GROUP IN A RECORDING SESSION. THE FINAL PARAGRAPH INDICATES A SUCCESSFUL RECORDING HAS BEEN MADE.) The recording engineer looks at the group. He smiles and punches the magic button on the Ampex again. The machine stops. The needle on the VU meter slumps. A career has started.

Not all feature stories are constructed using the circle technique, of course. Some stories build to a climactic ending. Others have a surprise ending.

TWENTY FIVE STORY TYPES

In the 1930s when the Hollywood studios were grinding out motion pictures like link sausages, some veteran screenwriters, pressed for time because of tight production schedules, turned to "plotwheels."

The plotwheels charted basic dramatic plots or storylines. Although there are hundreds of variations, the screenwriters claimed there were only three or four dozen basic plots. The screenwriters charted these plots and were able to develop hundreds of apparently varied scripts by merely inserting different character types and locations.

The premise of this portion of the guide is that both motion picture scripts and feature stories can be patterned.

What follows are the 25 most common feature story types. Some are also used by columnists.

There are more feature story types than these, of course, just as there were more plots than the basic three or four dozen used by some screenwriters in the heyday of film. Like the screenwriter's plotwheel, the feature story types are only points of beginning.

1. Advisory Story: Newspapers run many advisory features ranging from how to keep your health to how to fight city hall. The best such stories are written by experts who actually know how to keep their health or fight city hall.

A second best bet, as a reporter, is to actually experience an event and then write your impression of it, allowing readers to benefit from your experience. Example: You hire a lawyer to help fight a traffic ticket. After the trial you publish the lawyer's tips about the ins and outs of the legal system in your town.

The best advisory writing, even if experienced in the first person, is written in the second person plural, "you." The second person tends to create higher reader involvement.

2. Anniversary Story: The anniversary of a person, group, event or celebration is an excellent peg on which to hang a news feature. The usual practice is to compare and contrast the events that tie the past with the present. Example: You write a feature about a well-known hotel which is torn down the month it would have celebrated its 50th anniversary.

This is an Anniversary feature, using a descriptive lead. (All stories are by journalism students at the University of Arkansas at Little Rock and are reprinted with their permission.)

By JAN MEINS

The man stared at the pictures of gray ships on the living room wall, the hard lines of his jaw clenched tight as he recalled the painful memories undimmed by nearly four decades.

His stature, slightly bent with age and recent illness, remained proud and dignified. When he spoke, his voice sometimes wavered, remembering the bloody faces of comrades, the gagging smell of burning oil and flesh, the thunder of bombs and the roar of hundreds of airplanes.

"When we saw that rising sun, brother, we knew what was happening then," said Homer Hickey, 70, of Perryville, a retired Naval officer and survivor of the Japanese attack on Pearl Harbor on Dec. 7, 1941.

Hickey, 32 at the time of the attack, was a chief master of arms stationed aboard the U.S.S. Argonne. On the day of the attack, he had already spent 16 years in the Navy.

He intended to go ashore that morning in Honolulu with a friend who was teaching him to play golf.

"We met up on deck because we could not go ashore until after we ran our flag and colors at 8 a.m.," he said. "The first thing I noticed was a couple of planes coming over Ford Island, which is a seaplane base for the Navy.

"In just no time at all everything was flying into the air. We said, 'What the hell - the Army's out dropping smoke bombs again.' That's when we saw the rising sun on the wings of the planes and everybody took off for their gun stations.

"I was a gun captain on a five-inch gun. By the time we got to our stations, they were strafing the hell out of us," Hickey said. "Finally, finally we had some ammunition coming up to us on the deck.

"We looked down at the sub base harbor, and there came the real low torpedo planes. They were after the battleships, which were all lined up in perfect order.

"After 15 minutes, the battleships were throwing everything they had at the enemy planes."

During the battle, Hickey went out in a launch to pick up men in the water.

"Most of them were burning in the oil - the water was on fire - a lot of them had not had the experience to come up under the burning oil and knock the water away and get air. You could pick up a man and his whole scalp would come off in your hand," Hickey said.

"My launch got something entangled in the propeller and there we were - floating into the burning oil. We got over the side into the water and fixed it, and got back to the ship and I manned my gun again."

Hickey said he saw the U.S.S. Oklahoma capsize, the West Virginia, Tennessee and Nevada sink. But, he said, worst of all was what happened to the Arizona. It sank with more than 1,000 men below deck.

"They hit her ammo rooms; she blew all to pieces."

Near the end of the battle, Hickey remembers seeing the last wave of Japanese bombers coming down the channel.

"The last nine dive bombers - those sons-a-bitches - they were coming right at us, but then they went after the Nevada because she was the only one that had gotten underway during the attack. They hit her, but the old man (the Nevada's captain) got her out of the channel and beached her so we would not have a blocked channel," Hickey said.

Through the long day, the survivors rescued others and gathered up the wounded and the dead. The Oklahoma had overturned, and workers were trying to free men trapped inside. They went along the bottom of the ship and listened for tapping sounds from within.

Torches could not be used to cut through the steel for fear they might ignite the gas and oil, which was spilled everywhere, so they had to cut holes in the steel with air-driven chisels.

That evening, spatterings of gunfire could be heard. Men walked around stunned, performing mechanically whatever had to be done.

More than 1,000 survivors gathered in the mess hall of Hickey's ship, trying to find something to eat and a place to bed down for the night.

For some, though, the terror of the day was not over. Hickey said later that evening some American planes were accidentally fired upon by American ships.

"The guns followed our planes into the channel and hit our ship (the Argonne) and two or three other ships, killing some of our survivors," he said.

With the battle over and the long ordeal of four years of war just beginning, Hickey said he and the others waited for orders, bewildered, tired and sick of what they had seen of war.

"For three days I could not eat and didn't have any saliva in my mouth," Hickey said.

> For his actions at Pearl Harbor, Hickey was commissioned as a chief warrant officer in the United States Navy. Several days later, he was transferred to New Caledonia.
>
> Hickey and most of the 10,000 remaining survivors of Pearl Harbor are now in their 50's, 60's and 70's. But the years may never fade their memories of that day - 40 years ago today.

3. Autobiographical (or Eyewitness) Story: The writer writes in either the first or second person, describing his experiences to the reader. Example: At a plane crash with numerous fatalities, you record the sights and sounds of death in a vivid, first person, autobiographical sidebar.

4. Backgrounder Story: This type of feature, seen increasingly, explains and explores the background of something or someone in the news so that the reader may better understand his world. Example: You write a featurized account of the process of getting oil from the well to the neighborhood service station.

5. Behind-the-Scenes Story: Like the Backgrounder story, this may be either a news or time feature. The effect of this story depends upon the majority of your readers being unaware of how something dramatic or unusual is accomplished. Example: A firm in your town makes television commercials. You spend a day with the company and describe the production process to the readers.

> This Behind-the-Scenes story uses a descriptive lead. Note the use of the modified circle technique.
>
> By LINDA BENNETT
>
> The huge, gold and black cat let out a crescendo of bar-rattling roars as he paced fiercely from one end of his cage to the other.

When a long, slender animal prod was brought close to his cage, he lunged at it and roared again and again, with jaws open wide and teeth flashing.

Within a half hour, however, he was sleeping peacefully on the floor of his cage, looking for all the world like a big, loveable pussycat.

Jack, the male Siberian tiger at the Zoo of Arkansas, had been tranquilized—with great difficulty—for his annual physical examination. He was expected to sleep for at least two hours, to allow the medical team plenty of time to do its work.

The examination team for this year's physicals on the big cats consisted of a veterinarian, a dentist, the senior carnivore (meat-eaters) keeper, another keeper in the carnivore section, the zoo foreman, and a zoo volunteer working as a veterinary technician.

First, the tiger was weighed. With five men lifting him onto the scale, the verdict was 368 pounds.

Charting the weight is important, according to zoo director Bob Rooper, because it enables the staff to keep an eye on the growth and development of each animal from year to year.

Jim Eastbrook, zoo veterinarian, then drew a blood sample that would be tested for parasites, signs of anemia and infection, and would show how various organs were functioning.

Eastbrook quickly vaccinated the tiger for rabies, distemper, and upper respiratory virus, while the rest of the team also went to work.

The senior carnivore keeper used a large pair of hoof-nippers to trim the tiger's claws. Sometimes the claws don't wear normally in captivity, he explained, and they can curve under and cause infections.

Meanwhile, Steve Smith, a young dentist, went to work with a mallet and dental chisel to clean the tiger's teeth.

Smith, who spends most of his time as a "people dentist," was particularly interested in one of this tiger's teeth. During last year's physicals, Jack was found to have an abessed tooth. After unsuccessfully trying every means available to extract the tooth, Smith finally settled for performing a root canal on the animal, and he was anxious to see how it had worked out.

"It's okay," he said later, with a smile. "I'm really surprised."

Smith said he became interested in zoo dentistry when Eastbrook asked him to do some dental work on a 20-pound woolly monkey in the veterinarian's office. Smith was just out of dental school and had some extra time, so he obliged and has continued to help when he's needed.

"I'm not that active in clubs or other community activities, so I feel like this is a good way for me to help in the community," he said.

"What really sold me was working on the tiger last year. I realized how impressive these animals are," he said. "It's a change of pace for me," he said with a grin. "We have a good time.

"Sometimes I wish some of my people patients were more like these," he said with a laugh, stroking Jack's sleeping form.

As the dentist worked, other members of the team trimmed tangled clumps of fur, took the tiger's temperature—rectally—and checked him periodically for reflexes.

Tigers are particularly prone to convulsions when they are tranquilized, according to Eastbrook, the veterinarian, so they must be watched closely when they are "down."

Eastbrook makes regular rounds at the zoo one morning a week and is on 24-hour call for emergencies.

He talked convincingly about the need for regular, preventive veterinary service at the zoo, and he has spent more than three years working toward that goal.

"As people begin to believe there is a need for routine veterinary services, they begin to budget more for it," he said. With the cost of new zoo animals higher than ever, it has become even more important to keep those already owned healthy and productive.

A graduate of the Tuskegee Institute veterinary school in Alabama, Eastbrook said he is "totally self-taught" in zoo medicine. He estimated that about one-third of his time is spent on zoo matters, with the remaining time spent on his small animal and exotic pet practice in Little Rock.

As the team finished working with Jack, they cleared syringe caps, sponges and trash from his cage, and began preparations for the next patient - a 77 pound, female black leopard named Jezebel.

Under the watchful eyes of various team members, who would continue checking his breathing and reflexes until he woke up completely, Jack snoozed peacefully on, unaware that his appointment was over.

6. Case History Story: This story may or may not have a news peg. Either way, the story details the history of a person, group, event or institution. If the Case History deals with a person, you have a Personality Story. Case Histories of any type are the result of in-depth research. Documentation must be complete or the credibility of any future stories you may write is damaged.

The story may be antagonistic, middle-of-the road or favorable to the subject, depending upon the evidence exposed by the research.

Examples: (WITH A NEWS PEG) The mayor of

your town is forced to resign, so you write a feature about all previous mayors who have been forced to leave office, comparing the facts of their cases to the present one. (WITHOUT A NEWS PEG) You write an update feature on child adoption. The story traces the case history of a typical adoption from birth to entry into a local home.

This is a variation of the Case History, the Personality feature. It also has some Backgrounder characteristics. An astonisher lead is used.

By JO JACKSON

Caraleen Smith is a marked woman. She is marked so that she can live.

Her mark is reddish brown. It runs like a jagged scar forward from her right ear across the bottom of her jawbone to almost the middle of her chin.

It drops straight down to the hollow of her neck, slopes back to below the ear and up to where it began.

The mark outlines the area of her body undergoing radiation treatments for cancer at the Central Arkansas Radiation Therapy Institute in Little Rock.

"All of the patients have marks like mine, even though some may not be visible," she said. "The patients at CARTI identify with each other, not only because we have the little marks, but because of the atmosphere there."

Her large grey eyes are warm when she speaks of CARTI.

Mrs. Smith, 38, of North Little Rock, has Hodgkin's Disease.

She discovered a swelling beneath her right ear a few months ago. "After a few weeks, I went to our family doctor. He told me what it might be," she said.

"He referred me to a surgeon who removed the tumor. While I was in surgery, they did a biopsy, and the tumor was malignant.

"I was referred to a cancer specialist who diagnosed my disease as Hodgkin's Disease. He sent me to CARTI and to Dr. Langford."

Dr. Harold Langford is one of four radiotherapists with CARTI. He is chief of the medical staff, and "was actually with CARTI from the beginning," he said.

He emphasized that CARTI is a treatment center. They do not diagnose patients. Patients are sent for treatment by physicians from all over the state.

"There are three methods of treating cancer," Dr. Langford explained. "Usually there is surgery, but, often, to remove the malignancy completely would result in mutilation or serious cosmetic defects. So the surgery is combined with radiation therapy, which is what we do, or chemotherapy, or both.

"Most of our cases average from five to seven weeks of treatment. They must come in daily five days each week. It usually takes about 45 minutes to an hour for a visit. Some patients return at intervals for additional therapy, but for others, it is a one-time treatment. It depends on the case.

"In Caraleen's case, she has an excellent prognosis. She is in Stage 1-A, meaning the malignancy was confined and there is no systematic involvement.

"We have learned a lot in 25 years about Hodgkin's Disease. Back then, there were no survivors; people with Hodgkin's Disease were doomed.

"We just didn't understand the nature of the disease. It is still relatively uncommon. Cancer of the lungs, colon, are the big killers, and breast cancer in women."

Hodgkin's Disease is defined as one of the diseases of the lymphatic system. It is closely related to leukemia, and American Cancer Society reports include Hodgkin's Disease in the leukemia category.

"Cancer Statistics," published by the American Cancer Society, states that of 765,000 estimated new cancer cases in the United States this year, only 6,900 are expected to be Hodgkin's Disease.

The incidence is 7 percent for all lymphomas and leukemias in the United States, and deaths from these diseases comprise only 9 percent of all cancer deaths.

In Arkansas, an estimated 8,300 new cases of cancer will occur next year, of which only 300 are projected to be leukemia, which includes Hodgkin's Disease.

According to the Cancer Society, survival rates for Hodgkin's Disease are good. Figures are given only for all stages of the disease, which would include total involvement of the lymphatic system. The survival rate for males is 53 percent and for females 57 percent nationwide.

According to Dr. Langford, practically all lymphomas will be radiated at one time or another.

In the early stages, the disease is characterized by a painless enlargement of the lymph nodes, usually beginning in one side of the neck.

"There is really a message in Caraleen's case," Dr. Langford continued. "Here is a young woman who recognized that she had a disease early, and she did something about it.

"She was diagnosed early, treated early, and it is almost a sure thing that she will be cured."

During the past few months, as Caraleen Smith carried on her fight against cancer, she and her family have had many traumatic moments and difficult decisions to make.

Brushing back her dark brown hair, which falls in natural waves to her shoulders, she told her story in a voice which occasionally betrayed a hint of tears.

"The doctor told my husband, Roger, about the malignancy while I was still in surgery. Roger told me about it first, and then the doctor explained it to me.

"I don't use the word cancer. In my mind, it is associated with something fatal. My first reaction was I just didn't want anyone to know about it.

"I didn't want people to look at me differently or worry over me. I wanted them to look at the bright side of me. I shed a few tears, but I felt everything was going to be okay.

"My parents were Christians, and I have a deep faith. My husband is a minister, and I thought about a verse in the Bible. I thought if God's eye is on the sparrow, it is surely on me, also."

Mrs. Smith is a native of Malvern. Following her graduation from high school, she attended business school in Little Rock, and then worked as a secretary in Malvern for one year.

She met Roger Smith the next year when she went to Southwestern Assembly of God College in Waxahachie, Texas. She graduated from Southwestern, a two-year liberal arts college, as valedictorian of her class.

After her marriage to Smith more than 12 years ago, she worked as a bookkeeper in Dallas, and later in North Carolina, where Roger completed college and entered the ministry.

She stopped working when her first child, James Christian, now 8, was born. Her second child, Stephen Martin, was born four years later.

"I never planned to go back to work until the children were in school," Mrs. Smith said. "But after we moved to Arkansas five years ago, Roger decided to give up his position with the church. We now have a special Christian non-sectarian group that we work with, and Roger works full-time as a landscape contractor.

"So, when I learned that I would have to have surgery this summer, I knew we would have some serious financial concerns."

She explained that because she had rheumatic fever as a child, the cost of medical insurance for the family is prohibitive. So, they had nothing to pay medical bills with except their own resources.

"When I entered the hospital, they asked for $450 down. When I was dismissed, they wanted $915 more. We had money saved for a business investment and a modest savings of our own.

"When we added the bills from the doctors, we had spent more than $2,300 by the time I was to enter CARTI for treatment, and we had no money left to pay them."

Tears flooded her eyes, as she continued, her voice breaking from time to time.

"I called CARTI intending to ask how much it would cost per day and if they required it in advance because I knew we would have to make some arrangements.

"I just asked for information about this from the girl who answered the phone, and she asked who my doctor was. I told her my doctor would be Dr. Langford.

"I didn't ask to speak to him. I had never seen him, but he got on the phone to talk to me. I told him that I didn't want to bother him, but we didn't have insurance. I just wanted to know something before I came.

"He had my reports there. 'Mrs. Smith, do not stay away because of lack of money. What you have, we can cure,' he told me. He encouraged me to come, knowing we didn't have the money."

According to Margaret Holbert, who heads CARTI's social services department, the Smith's problems are quite common.

"By the time the patients come to us, they have all had many expenses. Cancer is an expensive disease. At least 95 percent of our patients have financial problems," she said.

"Our entire staff has had training in dealing with the emotional aspects of cancer. Our number one emphasis here is to treat the whole patient, and that means his psychological as well as his physical problems.

"Our section, which includes myself and case worker Mary McMan, who was assigned to work with the Smiths, usually has contact with every patient at some time or another.

"The number one problem is usually financial, but since the majority of our patients are from outside central Arkansas, we also assist with housing, transportation, counseling, and other family problems which affect the patient's adjustment to his disease and his treatment."

Edward Arthur Jr., executive director of CARTI, outlined the six-year history and philosophy of the center. Funds for the original construction came from a bond issue. CARTI is a non-profit corporation and receives both private and public funds.

An expansion program is now scheduled. CARTI will add a dental department with two treatment rooms and a lab, a small auditorium for teaching purposes and an additional high energy Clinac 20 machine.

Mrs. Smith is undergoing treatment on the Clinac 18, which is a deep penetrating machine. The machine is complex and expensive, and it needs repairs, or adjustments. At present, there is no backup machine for the C-18.

The addition of the Clinac 20 will provide backup, and also allow for treatments which are not currently done.

CARTI has a policy of turning away no one. If no source of help can be found for a patient, a portion of the expenses may be paid from funds made available by the CARTI Auxiliary, which regularly has fund raising activities in addition to its contribution of volunteer hours with the patients.

According to Miss Holbert, CARTI staff is usually successful in financially assisting patients through one of several sources.

First, there is third-party insurance. In cases such as Mrs. Smith's, where the patient has a prospect of going back to work, the Rehabilitation Services Division of the Arkansas Human Services Department, will pay for treatment and other expenses.

For older patients, Medicare pays, and if the family has no resources, Medicaid will pay for 100 percent of the treatment.

The American Cancer Society helps with supplies for patients. "We use all the resources we know to help our patients," Miss Holbert said.

"In the Smith's case, they could not qualify for Medicaid, so we called on the rehabilitation counselor to work with them."

Mrs. Smith continued. "My husband went with me on my first visit to see Dr. Langford. We were concerned about the total effects of the x-rays. Dr. Langford explained the treatment to us and told us, in my case, there was no alternative treatment.

"After I had been under a machine to be marked up, they told me Mary McMan, the case worker, wanted to see me. She explained the Rehabilitation Services program to us. She said it was for people who will be able to go back to work.

"She knew I had not worked in some years, and she wanted to know my plans.

"I told her that I had always wanted to be an elementary education teacher. But first, I am a mother. I want to go back to college after my 4-year-old gets in school, which will be next fall.

"Mary called a rehabilitation counselor in to work with me. My counselor sent me for an examination by a Rehabilitation Services doctor. Then, I was given a written test. It was a college entrance exam."

Mrs. Smith's eyes were happy again, and she smiled brightly. "I understand I did really well on it," she said. "It was very stimulating and interesting.

"My counselor told me that they had set aside a special amount of money for me. My treatments would be paid for, and if I would enter the University of Arkansas at Little Rock next fall, Rehabilitation Services will pay my tuition for me to complete my college education.

"My husband and I talked all of this out. We had our own goals set, and I wanted to be with the children until they started to school. Above all, we did not want to take anything we were not eligible for.

"We talked with the people at CARTI and Rehabilitation Services about our goals as a family unit. We wanted everything out front."

The fact that CARTI has been able to help the Smiths is not unintentional. According to Arthur, "We work hard at being an institution with a heart."

Dr. Langford said that CARTI's entire physical plant and furnishings were planned to produce an atmosphere of calmness and comfort. He and others traveled to several such facilities in the United States while CARTI was still in the planning stage.

"Our offices were decorated by a professional decorator. The colors, the recessed lighting, the green plants ...everything was designed to make it comfortable for the patients.

"There is no hard data on what we know to be a fact," he said, "and that is that the psychological aspects of cancer and the treatment are very important in the prognosis of the patient."

As for Caraleen Smith, she is an enthusiastic supporter of the CARTI staff. "The receptionist was able to call me by my first name after the second visit," she said. "We visit with other patients in the waiting room, and volunteers are there to assist us and talk with us.

"When you have our disease, all social status and economic status are stripped away. We know we are all there because we hope to be helped.

"I have wanted to help as I have been helped. I talked with one patient who lived a long ways away, and she was having a three-hour drive each day. Her husband was taking off from work to bring her.

"I told her that I didn't have a big, fancy house, but I would be glad for her to come stay with me. That was on Friday, and I called on Sunday to let her know I really meant it. We are lifelong friends now."

For Caraleen Smith, the awesome, black cloud which menaced her life and threatened her family's future a few weeks ago has lifted.

The mark, too, will gradually fade away in time.

"What has happened to me is unbelievable," she said. "I thought I couldn't afford to go to CARTI for treatment unless we made a great sacrifice, and here I am going to college.

"I know God's eye is on me, and I'm going to be all right."

7. Collector Story: This is a traditional feature story, used too often by most newspapers. Typically, the writer interviews a collector of unusual items about his hobby. Example: You interview a local man who has the largest collection of stuffed aardvarks in your state.

This is a modified version of the Collector feature. A contrast and comparison lead is used.

By JO JACKSON

A rusting hulk of metal tubing shaped like a giant grasshopper rests in Winston Evans' backyard.

To anyone else, it looks like junk. To Evans, it looks like a blueprint for building an airplane.

The rusting hulk is a fusilage of a Taylor Craft L-2M. The single engine Taylor Craft was built in the 1940s as a military reconnaissance plane.

"I have never seen this model in flying condition," Evans says, "but I talked to some folks about it. They told me there weren't many of them built."

Evans admits that building an airplane in his backyard is not going to be easy. Right now, he can't do much on the construction because he doesn't have a building large enough to house it.

"I've been intending to put up a building," he says, "but I've had too many other things going on this summer."

Evans lives off Colonel Glen Road in western Pulaski County. He works as an automobile body repairman for a body shop in Little Rock.

Evans has never built a plane. He has had flying lessons, but doesn't have a pilot's license.

"I helped a friend build one," he says. "I'm sure I can do it.

"You know," he says, "I grew up on a farm near Shirley, Arkansas. In Shirley, we didn't take our equipment or machinery to town to have it fixed. If it broke down, we fixed it ourselves."

He says he came by this plane by helping someone out. "I repaired this fellow's car for him and he gave me the plane," he says. It is a retired crop duster, he explains.

"When this plane was first built, it had windows on each side of the enclosed cockpit," Evans says. Indicating a section along the top with his finger, he continues, "There was a window on the top above the cabin here. They called the plane 'The Greenhouse.' "

Much of "The Greenhouse" is stored in a machinery shed crammed with equipment and parts. Evans points out the motor, the wheels, the instrument panel and other assorted pieces of the plane.

"I think I can pretty well use the wheels like they are," he says. "I could rebuild the motor if I can find a shaft that will fit it."

The 14-foot wings are stored under the house, as is the tail section. Evans thinks they are sound and will only need recovering.

Evans and his wife, Carolyn, have measured and marked each piece of the metal tubing of the fusilage. He has drawn a blueprint showing how each piece fits with others.

Using catalogues for aircraft supply houses, Evans has calculated the tubing alone will cost $470.

"The reason I can't put it together here in the open," continues Evans, "is because the tubing will rust from rain. Before I weld the tubing into a new frame, I have to drill holes for fittings.

"Water will get in the holes, and when it freezes, the tubing will burst. So the fusilage will have to be assembled indoors."

Evans is undaunted by the complexities of building a plane.

He says constructing an airplane is right in line with his training in radio and electronics maintenance and auto repairs. However, he admits that building a plane isn't the only problem. There's also the problem of finding the time to work.

"If I had the place and the time," he says, "I could finish the plane in about six months, working three or four hours a day....I calculate it will cost about $3,000 to build it," he says.

He gives the rusty fusilage a final pat and looks up in the sky. In his mind's eye, Evans isn't seeing a rusty hulk of metal tubing. He's seeing a graceful "Greenhouse," soaring among the clouds. With himself at the controls, naturally.

8. Colloquy Story: Used more for columns than features, this story uses a point-counterpoint dialogue comparing two or more opposing viewpoints. The opposing dialogue can be interwoven by using transitions with direct, indirect and partial quotations. Example: You join two politicians of violently opposing views and question them on the issues in their campaign. The story is written to include the setting of the meeting--a bar, bowling alley, television studio or local restaurant.

9. Composite Picture Story: From a statistical survey, such as one from the Census Bureau or Federal Bureau of Investigation, you create a composite picture of an average person, group, situation, city or event. Example: Rapes are increasing in your town. Using the latest FBI reports and local police files, you reconstruct the typical rape.

10. Decalog Story: This feature story uses a list of 10 as a basis for evaluation. Variations on the Decalog include 10 places to vacation in your home state, 10 reasons to repair the family car yourself, the 10 best movies of the year and 10 worst potholes in your city streets.

A variation is the Enumeration Story where fewer or more than 10 items are listed.

11. Dialogue Story: Occasionally feature pieces--but usually columns--may be written

totally in real or fictitious dialogue, in order to reveal cahracter. Example: The local political situation in your town is the subject of a feature written entirely from the overheard conversation of two men in a locker room. (A variation of this is to use just a short amount of the dialogue to tease the reader into the story.)

12. Diary Story: A diary is a frank record of daily events, usually not intended for publication. Written in sentence fragments and the second person, this feature story type can be effective if used rarely. Example: Using a diary approach, you write a feature about your efforts to get a regional gasoline credit card accepted on a cross-country trip during a fuel shortage.

13. Different Views Story: Five people see the same event in five different ways, i.e., a minister, lawyer, student, teacher and housewife may all have different views on a teacher strike. As a feature writer, you can take a current event and write about it from the multi-view perspective of a number of different citizens, liberally using quotations and description.

A variation of this story type, usually without transitions, is the Man-On-The-Street interview.

14. Dying Person Story: You interview a dying person, preferably a child, about his wishes, hopes and dreams. Usually the story is pegged to a donation request to help defray huge medical expenses. Example: A dying boy, who hopes to be a musician, is interviewed. The readers know he will never live to fulfill his dream.

This is a Dying Person feature, with a long, modified, irony lead.

BY AMY BURCHAM

Petite, blue-eyed Monica Angelique Edward will be celebrating her fourth birthday on Aug. 11. Her birthday wish is for a trip to Disney World in

33

Orlando, Fla., on July 11, during her father's only vacation time this year.

Watching his lovable, fragile daughter playing with her latest new toy - one of which she receives almost daily - Gene Edward, her father, wants Monica's every wish fulfilled, including this birthday wish.

Her father isn't spoiling her because Monica's fourth birthday may be her last. She has neuroblastoma, a cancer in her bone marrow that is in its final stage.

Her parents, Gene, 32, and Juanita Edward, 31, of Little Rock, have been told by their daughter's physician the Monica has less than one year to live.

If you asked Monica who she would be going to see, she would gleefully answer, "Donald Duck an' Mickey Mouse."

Her heart is set on the trip and so is her father's. "She's gonna go no matter what because that's what she wants," Mr. Edward said.

Monica's aunt, Mrs. Betty Jones of Benton, has taken charge of the fund raising campaign to fulfill Monica's wish.

"The idea about the trip started when she was in the hospital three weeks ago. We put a piggy bank in her room and all the family started putting money in there whenever they came by," Mrs. Jones said.

"The family has given $800 and after a short article ran in the newspaper June 19 we got $173," Mrs. Jones said.

"Some people have just sent one dollar with the nicest letters. It's really nice to read some of the letters we've gotten. Sometimes checks just come in an envelope with no name. We really appreciate all the people that have given so far," Mrs. Jones said.

Mr. Edward said they have estimated the cost of the trip at $2,500 for five people. Mr. and Mrs. Edward, along with their 8-year-old daughter, Kim, and Mrs. Edwards 15-year-old sister, Penny, will be making the trip.

"Penny is going along because I need her to help me take care on Monica because she gets real fussy sometimes," Mrs. Edward said.

Monica wasn't real fussy until three short weeks ago when her neuroblastoma was diagnosed.

"I had taken Juanita to the dentist," Mrs. Jones said, "and was sitting in the waiting room with Monica. I noticed she was running a fever and she told me her jaw was hurting. I went to tell her mother that we needed to get home soon because this child has a fever," Mrs. Jones said.

According to Monica's mother, the dentist took an x-ray that day but didn't see anything.

"He referred us to a pediatric oral surgeon for more x-rays," Mrs. Edward said. "We had an appointment for Tuesday, but that weekend her jaw started to swell and one of her secondary molars turned black and I thought it was an abscessed tooth. I called the oral surgeon and he told me to bring Monica in Monday to admit her to the hospital for oral surgery.

"He took a biopsy on Tuesday morning and Wednesday we were told that the growth was malignant, but we didn't get the complete pathology report until Thursday. That's when we were referred to Arkansas Children's Hospital," Mrs. Edward said.

"The next day (Friday) we were told by the doctor that the cancer had spread into her bone marrow and Monica had less than one year to live," Mrs. Edward said.

During Monica's stay at the hospital all reports said she was a doll.

"She called her IVs (intravenous feeding tubes) her 'rig.' When she wanted to go somewhere she would say, 'Daddy, get my rig,' " her aunt recalled.

Monica is at home with her family now. Just watching her play and talk, you would never know she's sick.

But, she is receiving radiation treatment and will begin

> chemotherapy as soon as she returns from Disney World.
> "We're trying to raise the money for the trip to Disney World for Monica. This trip will do her well because it will take her mind off of really hurtin'," Mr. Edward said.

15. Fable Story: A fable is a fictitious narrative involving a moral (normally at the end) designed to illustrate a life lesson. Fables feature animals as characters. If you want to use people as characters in your story or more likely, in your column, you are writing a parable. Example: You translate the local political frontrunners into tortoise and hare types.

16. Glossary Story: Glossaries are specialized dictionaries of jargon. Feature stories are often written using or explaining the jargon of a sub-culture, such as the drug culture.

17. Handicapped Person Story: Usually in every community, a handicapped person is making a living in an unusual way. Example: A blind woman paints ashtrays and sells them at the town bus station.

18. Man-From-Outer-Space Story: This story approach uses observations from a visitor unfamiliar with a local situation or custom. Example: You write a feature about a visiting Soviet journalist and record his comments about unemployment in your town.

19. Manual Story: Rarely used, this type of feature, or column, adopts the manual technique of explaining a simple action. Example: With humor, and as it would be written in an instruction manual, you explain how to enroll for a night class at the local college.

20. Most-Unusual-Way-To-Make-A-Living Story: In every city, at least several dozen people have unusual occupations that put them in danger daily. Many others have jobs that are humorous or disgusting. Example: You interview a window washer on the job at a tall building.

This Most-Unusual-Way-To-Make-A-Living feature uses a descriptive lead. Note the liberal uses of quotes to tell the story of Allen Barberry.

By RODNEY BOWERS

Allen Barberry rubbed the gray stubble on his face and pulled a woolen cap to his head as he shuffled his 48-year-old frame into the kitchen for the day's first cup of coffee.

The sun was slowly lifting the fog over North Little Rock as he made ready to run his traps another day.

Barberry has been an outdoorsman as long as he can remember.

He received no formal education, but he said he "learnt the ways of nature" from the backwoods and swamps of central Arkansas.

"My daddy taught me how to trap when I was six. Daddy would take a piece of salt meat and a biscuit and put it in his pocket for me. He'd leave me a stump and go out in the woods," he recalled. His father, Barberry said, would return "much later" bringing back "many a tale," another welcome biscuit and a stomach-pleasing piece of salt meat.

The life of an outdoorsman isn't spent "jest hunting and fishing," and Barberry let his thoughts drift back to adventures of younger days and told of the time his father and uncles were living in a camp.

"They put dough in my Uncle Jess' 'Long Tom' shotgun and told him he couldn't kill a bird sittin' yonder in a tree. He nearly kilt himself. He blowed his gun up and blacked his eye," he said, chuckling.

He also remembered how his uncle "paid 'em back. He spread out black powder where they had coffee and gravy on the table and took a hot wire to it and blowed it up on them."

Barberry also recalled his brothers' finding two wild pups abandoned in a dead cow's stomach. Apparently, he said, the mother left them there knowing they would have a source of food. "They was mixed with coyote or wolf. My momma was the only one who could touch 'em," Barberry said.

From his years of trapping, Barberry said, he has come to "know about everything that ever walked."

He once trapped a "critter," but he wasn't quite sure what it was. "It was one of the prettiest ones I ever seen. It was a black cat that looked like a fox. I thought it looked like a panther, but it wasn't. They (the Arkansas Game and Fish Commission) called it a ferret cat. I'd give anything to have had it mounted. He stood that dad-burned high"—he indicated 30 inches with his calloused hand.

The ferret cat wasn't the only unusual animal Barberry has happened upon during his 40 years of trapping and fishing near his Sylvan Hills home.

"We use to catch red fox on the (Arkansas) river but the coyotes have kil't them all," he said. "I only seen two fox tracks this year, but I've seen anywhere 'tween one and six coyotes a day."

Barberry also takes note of other Arkansas wildlife he encounters.

"Just the other day, I seen some blue cranes—herons—below England (Ark.). They use to be on the river, but you never see them like that, no more."

Barberry said he spends almost as much time fishing the river as he does trapping.

Digging through his wallet, Barberry produced an impressive picture of a 6-foot, 9-inch gar fish weighing "right near 200 pounds," which he caught in the Arkansas River.

"He put it—the gar—in my bathtub and tried to revive it," Pat Barberry, Allen's wife, said while shaking her head in disbelief.

Fond memories don't lie just in Barberry's past.

"I can show you where whiskey stills is right now," he said with a sly grin.

"It ain't like it was, anymore," Barberry said thoughtfully.

Weather and water situations aren't quite the same now, according to Barberry.

"I remember walking across the (Arkansas) river when it was frozen during the late 30's," he said.

"It's getting that cold again."

Draining the swamps around the area of North Little Rock—once known as Huntersville—has hurt the animals, Barberry said.

"They're getting all the timber out and the freeways are killing more animals than the trappers," Barberry said, wagging his head like a great bear.

"Dry weather kills all the animals, but the beavers help these here animals. Nature's going to take care of itself," he said.

Barberry is so determined nature will provide for her own, he has taught his four boys the "art" of trapping.

"I don't have any daughters, but I got a grand-daughter," he said.

Barberry thought about his grand-daughter becoming a trapper, paused a moment, then said with a smile: "My momma was a trapper."

21. New Business Story: Some newspapers don't run these stories. Most do (usually under the guise of business page copy). Be careful. If this type of story is handled poorly, you will have a boring puff piece which will be read avidly only by the owner of the new business. But, if handled skillfully, these stories may provide real entertainment and information.

If the story is about the owner or an employee of the business, you have a Personality feature; but if the angle is about what the business sells (man-eating fish), makes (factory-built homes) or buys to re-sell (ants, so they can be covered with chocolate, sealed in tins and sold for $20 a can), you probably have a traditional New Business feature.

If you find a real news peg (example: an anti-freeze shortage), you'll have an even better reason to write this kind of story. In the case of a news peg, the business really need not be new, so long as the tie to the peg is obvious (an anti-freeze manufacturing company expanding to meet needs).

> This is a modified New Business feature, using a descriptive lead. Note that the business is not new, only unusual.

By KAY CROSS TOOLE

Seventeen miles south of Pine Bluff on U.S. 65 is a small farm community called Monroe.

Surrounded by vast acres of rich farming land, the farmers there grow row groups such as cotton, soybeans and rice.

One farmer at Monroe, however, decided to raise a different kind of crop. He is a fish farmer.

Dr. Earl E. Burns, owner of Burns and Sons Farms, has been raising fish since 1968. The fish farm's initial development began in 1967 with the construction of 17 acres in ponds.

Today there are 29 ponds—128 acres—on the Burns' farm. Dr. Burns, who has a Ph.D. in higher education, raises catfish fingerlings, catfish as a food fish and minnows.

Dr. Burns, 65, reviewed his 12 years of experience in the fish farming industry and talked about his success, his failures, his regrets, and his hopes for the future.

"This is a very expensive operation. There are problems you wouldn't envision," Dr. Burns said. A look of seriousness spread over his face.

From 1944-68 Dr. Burns was a row crop farmer. He also was employed by what is now the University of Arkansas at Pine Bluff. While he was employed by the college, he came across various reading material that told about the catfish industry, then a relatively new one.

"I got into the business because of the material I read," Dr. Burns said. He also said he was informed by others that fish farming was a profitable enterprise.

Commercial fish farming dates back to the 1920s. Its development began on the delta lands of Arkansas, Mississippi, and Louisiana, where 80 percent of the industry may still be found, according to Dr. Burns.

Commercial fish farming as an industry did not begin to emerge until the 1940s. Delta farmers began focusing considerable attention on commercial production of catfish in the 1960s, following an unsuccessful attempt at growing buffalo in rotation with rice, Dr. Burns said.

Arkansas now leads the nation in commercial fish farming, ranking second behind Mississippi in the production of catfish.

The Burns' farm was featured in the October, 1968, issue of "Ebony" magazine, where it was reported to be the first fish farm in Arkansas on which a fish processing plant was built.

In the same issue, "Ebony" reported that Burns and Sons had invented an automatic catfish feeder on which a patent was granted in 1970.

The processing plant is closed now. "It proved to be unprofitable," Dr. Burns said.

In fact, a lot of things have changed on the Burns farm since 1968. Dr. Burns runs the business by himself now. His three sons have left home and entered other careers.

He lives alone in a mobile home located on the farm, which has lost some of the appearance of a thriving industry.

Dr. Burns sells his fingerlings (4-6 inch, or 6-8 inch catfish) to markets in Missouri, Kentucky, Illinois, Mississippi, Alabama and Texas.

He sells his food fish to live haulers who sell them to lake owners in Missouri, Ohio, Pennsylvania and Kentucky.

The minnows are sold mostly to out-of-state dealers (Kentucky, Missouri and Texas), but some are sold to bait shops in Pine Bluff and northern Arkansas.

"The fact that I don't sell my fish locally has hurt my popularity somewhat," Dr. Burns said, "but I just can't afford to.

"This business is characterized with high capital costs and high risks," Dr. Burns said.

"The primary risk is the loss of oxygen in hot water." Dr. Burns said he had seen entire crops of fish die quickly from this problem.

The development of an aerator, a device which shoots the pond water up in the air, thus supplying it with new oxygen, has remedied this problem somewhat, but not entirely, according to Dr. Burns.

Perhaps Dr. Burns' biggest complaint about the fish farming industry is the fact that government agencies won't make loans to fish farmers like they do for other farmers.

"It takes an awful lot of money," Dr. Burns said. "It costs from $2,500 to 3,000 to put one acre in shape, then it costs anywhere from $1,000 to $1,500 to put an acre in operation."

Dr. Burns does acknowledge the fact that fish farming provides the highest income per acre of any agricultural crop, but like most businessmen, fish farmers have to have money to make money.

"I don't think government agencies could justify their abstinence from giving loans to fish farmers. There should be some orderly agency to provide finances to fish farmers," Dr. Burns said.

Dr. Burns said he felt that in the future some government agencies would start making loans to fish farmers. "I think the future holds a lot for the fish industry."

A well known person in the catfish industry, Dr. Burns served this past year as Aquaculture Coordinator for the USDA and had devoted much of his time to researching the future of the fish farming industry.

According to Dr. Burns, farm-raised catfish accounts for nearly 3 percent of the total fish harvest in the U.S., and as the industry matures and operates more efficiently, fish farms promise to become even more important food providers.

The industry could conceivably grow to 10 times its present size by the year 2000, he said.

Dr. Burns has provided consultant assistance to fish farmers and corporations in Arkansas, Alabama, Georgia, Mississippi and South Carolina.

In 1970, he was employed by the Ford Foundation of New York to do a feasibility study of an application for funds to develop a fish farming project in Georgia. He later headed the team of designers for that project.

"I've enjoyed working with catfish. I have probably enjoyed as good a reputation as anyone in the United States in fish farming," said Dr. Burns.

However, even with a successful business, Dr. Burns admitted that he occasionally regrets getting into the fish farming business. "Life would have been a lot easier if I hadn't," he said.

22. New Invention Story: Many people are basement inventors. Once in a while, these people come up with a startling, and newsworthy idea. Such ideas usually make excellent feature copy. Example: A man in your town invents a new way to squeeze out all the toothpaste from a toothpaste tube.

23. Open Letter Story: Although primarily a column device, successful feature stories are occasionally written in this format. The stories are aimed at bringing inside information to the reader or explaining a viewpoint held by a local group or organization to a public personality (for instance, the governor of your state). Example: You (assuming the identity of an automobile tire) write a letter to county road officials complaining about potholes.

A variation of the Open Letter feature or column is the Memorandum Story, which purports to be a memo from an insider of an organization to its chief officer. Both the Open Letter and Memorandum stories are to one degree or another somewhat fictional and should be clearly identified as such.

24. Resurrected Story: With this story type, a recent news event provides a peg to bring a long buried story into the daylight again. Example: A road-building crew discovers the bones of an Indian family. You contact the local historical society for a story about Indian history in your area.

25. Stunt Story: This story type is perhaps one of the oldest but most fertile fields on the feature farm.

Using this approach, the writer assumes the role of a football player, beggar, drug pusher, or garbage man in order to write a story of life in that sub-culture.

The story is different from the Behind-the-Scenes feature in that the writer actually submerges into the sub-culture rather than acting as an impartial observer. Example: You go into spring practice with the local college football team to write about the deprivations they experience.

FEATURE LEADS

The lead entices the reader into the feature story and captures his interest. The lead also sets the tone of the story. Leads, like one ant attacking the potato salad at a picnic, can't do the job alone. The lead is only part of a whole and needs adept writing along with an effective story idea to make the feature work well.

The following leads are examples of the most commonly used types. Variations abound. Create your own and mix them freely with story types.

1. Allusion Lead, Literary or Historical: This lead attempts to tie in the theme of the feature story with a literary or historical event, comparing and contrasting the two. Example: (HISTORICAL, REGARDING A MAN WHO TRIED TO DEFEND HIMSELF IN COURT) Custer fought his last stand 100 years ago. Henry Yarrow fought his yesterday.

2. Astonisher Lead: Also called a punch or cartridge lead, the astonisher sums up in a startling, often contradictory approach, the sum of the story. Example: (REGARDING A MAN WHO BUILT A GLIDER IN HIS BASEMENT) John Williams always wanted to soar like a bird. Tuesday he did.

3. Blind Lead: Here the writer delays identification of a person, group or event. He may use the suspended interest form, delaying identification until the end of the story, or he may reveal identity in the lead. Example: The man shifted on his feet uneasily. He looked at the crowd in front of him. He tapped the microphone to see if it was working. The president-elect of the United States was ready to speak.

4. Box Score Lead: This approach is sometimes used to sum up the context of a complicated event in a few words. Example: (REGARDING A POLICE SHOOT-OUT WITH BANK ROBBERS) Police, three. Bankrobbers, none.

5. Cause-Effect Lead: Here a cause is linked to an effect. If the cause is old and the effect is new, the result is an anachronism. Example: Henry Ford's industrial engineers told him the answer to high manufacturing costs was something called an assembly line. Last week at Lordstown, Ohio, where subcompact Chevrolets are made, General Motors was cursing that concept.

6. Contrast and Comparison Lead: Essentially, this lead is the same kind of creature as the Cause-Effect lead, with the difference that the Contrast and Comparison lead compares items of a like nature, whether they are related in time or not. Example: (REGARDING A RADIO ANNOUNCER) Peter Harrison is a little like an alarm clock. He has to wake people up - 100,000 people every morning.

7. Descriptive Lead: With this lead, you simply describe something. Example: (REGARDING THE EFFECTS OF MARIJUANA) The house smelled, smelled like 100 feet of mildewed rope had been burned in the living room. The ceiling stank, the couch reeked. Samson sat back into the deeply upholstered chair, puffed on a funny looking little cigarette, and blew more smell into the room.

8. Dialogue Lead: Dialogue, usually quoted out of context from within the body of the story, is used to tease the audience into reading the feature. The dialogue is often set in boldface or italic type, then repeated later in the story.

9. Diary Lead: The diary technique, keeping a daily record for a period of time, is sometimes used to dramatically begin a feature. Example: Tuesday the 19th of June. Met the President of the United States today.

10. Direct Address Lead: In this instance, the writer, without using direct quotes, addresses the reader. Example: (REGARDING RUNAWAY CHILDREN) Relax, kids. You have a friend at the Denver police station.

11. Enumeration Lead: This lead lists, or enumerates, the facts or figures relative to a story. Example: The Dodgers won it that time,

18 to 4. It was the only time that season.

   12. Epigram Lead: This one, thankfully, is used rarely. An epigram is a short, witty saying. The epigram lead is a short, witty line usually tied to a matching sentence comparing or contrasting the epigram. Example: (REGARDING AN ACCOUNTANT WHO RUNS A ROCK SHOP) A rolling stone gathers no moss. Frank Moss, on the other hand, gathers stones for a living.

   13. Irony Lead: The irony lead is the heaviest weapon in the arsenal of style. Irony spotlights the difference between things as they should be and things as they are. Example: The President of the United States spoke Tuesday about governmental belt tightening efforts during the current inflationary siege. Wednesday he flew to Colorado for a vacation. Cost to taxpayers: $57,000.

   14. Onomatopoeia Lead: Onomatopoeia means a word that sounds like a sound--"buuzzzzz" for a saw operating, "moooooo" for a cow doing whatever a cow does. This lead type is often used to open a feature when your story material is basically dull.

   15. Parody Lead: This lead is similar to the epigram lead, but uses a parody instead. A parody--in this case--is often a satirical imitation of a line in a motion picture, book or musical composition.

   16. Prediction Lead: Simply, the lead predicts a future event. Example: The automobile airbag will eventually replace the seat belt in your family car, according to the people who know the automobile safety business.

   17. Question Lead: This lead uses a question, often in the form of a direct, indirect or partial quote, to begin the feature story.

   18. Quote Lead: In this lead type, an attributed quote, either direct, indirect or partial, opens the feature. Description is also used. Example: (REGARDING THE COST OF OPERATING AN AUTOMOBILE) The service station owner leaned back into his chair and puffed a Winston. "I

don't like to say it," he said nonetheless, "but I see the price of gas going up to $7 a gallon in the next three years."

    19. Second Person Plural Lead: This lead, often used with Autobiographical story types, requires that the writer begin his story in the second person plural. Example: You've always wondered what the inside of a Minuteman missile site looked like. Yesterday you found out.

    20. Staccato Lead: This lead uses a series of sentence fragments--the same kind that used to infuriate your high school English teacher--to tie together a description of a person, group, place or event. Use staccato sparingly. Example: The smack of leather against horseflesh. The crackle of the public address system. A thud of ground being slapped. The snap of a rider's leg. Those are the sounds of rodeo.

POSTSCRIPT

You know most of the tricks of the trade now--the techniques, the story types and lead variations. All you have to do is find a feature idea and construct your story. If you marry the suggestions in this guide with good reporting skills (primarily interviewing), you'll be on your way toward mastering feature writing.

There are, however, five additional tips worth passing along.

● Read feature stories in the local papers. Dissect them for additional literary techniques and story and lead variations.

● Sharpen your sense of the dramatic and the ironic. Most features, at heart, deal with offbeat slices of life.

● Learn to develop an ear for the way people speak (and at the same time an unobtrusive manner of notetaking).

● Become an expert interviewer. (Sorry, there are no easy ways; you learn this by experience.)

● Learn to like people. If you don't, you're in the wrong business.